IMAGES
of America

HIGH UINTAS
WILDERNESS

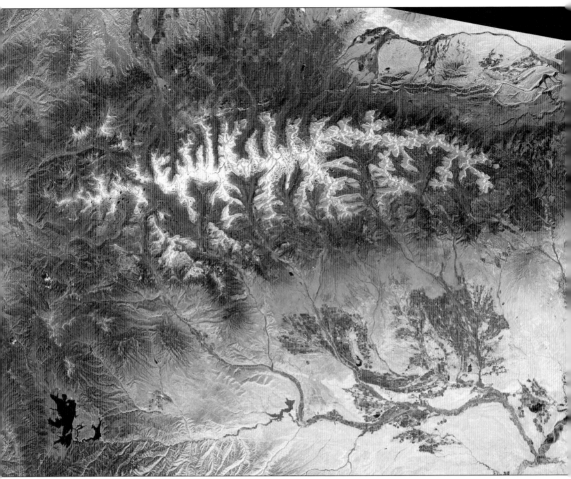

This photograph, taken from orbit, shows new snow on the Uinta Mountains on July 15, 2011. Snow can fall in any month of the year in this 10,000- to 13,500-foot elevation range. Note the rare east-west trend of these mountains, as they are the only major mountains in the lower 48 states that do not run north and south. (Courtesy of NASA's Earth Observatory.)

ON THE COVER: Five unidentified members of the Wasatch Mountain Club, including three women, converse after hiking to the summit of Hayden Peak in July 1931. Ryder Lake is shown below, and Kletting Peak is in the distance. (Courtesy of J. Willard Marriott Digital Library, the University of Utah.)

IMAGES
of America

HIGH UINTAS
WILDERNESS

Lynn Arave

ARCADIA
PUBLISHING

Published by Arcadia Publishing
Charleston, South Carolina

Printed in the United States of America

Library of Congress Control Number: 2024940995

For all general information, please contact Arcadia Publishing:
Telephone 843-853-2070
Fax 843-853-0044
E-mail sales@arcadiapublishing.com

Visit us on the Internet at www.arcadiapublishing.com

To my High Uintas hiking partners–Wayne Arave, Roger Arave, Ravell Call, Ray Boren, Steven Arave, Taylor Arave, Russell Arave, Jake Arave, Daniel Hafen, Liz Arave Hafen, Scott Wesemann, and Craig Lloyd. Plus, my loyal canine companions–Wolfe, Snickers, and Henrie.

CONTENTS

ACKNOWLEDGMENTS

Special thanks to all the sources that allowed use of their historical images for this book. These include the Utah State Historical Society, the J. Willard Marriott Digital Library at the University of Utah, Uintah County Library Regional History Center, Library of Congress, New York Public Library, Brigham Young University Lee Library, NASA's Earth Observatory, Smithsonian National Portrait Gallery, National Archives, Delta Library, Deseret News Archives, and the Salt Lake Tribune Archives.

Friends and family who supplied pictures for this book are Ravell Call, Roger Arave, Whitney Arave, LeAnn Arave, and Liz Arave Hafen.

Also, a special thanks to the Wasatch Mountain Club for making sure that its historic photographs were preserved from the early 20th century. Without them, this book would not have been possible.

INTRODUCTION

The Uinta Mountains/High Uintas, located in northeastern Utah, are a unique natural treasure for the state. While some of Utah's national parks—like Zion, Bryce, Arches, etc.—garner the most international publicity, the Uintas remain an uncrowded western wilderness that many outsiders have never heard of.

In fact, even Sir Edmund Hillary, one of the first two men to climb Mount Everest, found the pristine Uinta Mountains a delight in his two visits.

The Uinta name comes from a Ute word that means "pine forest" or "pine tree."

The Mormon pioneers had obviously noticed the snowcapped Uinta Mountains in early July 1847, when they traversed by Fort Bridger in today's Wyoming en route to today's Utah.

However, with only a tolerable climate in the summer, the Uintas were not permanently colonized by the pioneers or even modern man. Indeed, the closest year-round outposts in the Uintas are Bear River Station on the east side; the town of Kamas on the west; Lonetree, Wyoming, on the north; and various Uinta Basin communities, like Vernal, on the south end. Evanston, Wyoming, is the largest city north of the Uintas.

The High Uintas contain timber resources as well as wildlife resources. However, the greatest natural resource in the Uintas is water. The area is a significant water generator for three states—Utah, Wyoming, and Idaho. The Uintas contain the headwaters for the Bear River as well as the Weber, Provo, and Duchesne Rivers.

In fact, there is a six-mile-long underground canal in the Uintas, which diverts water from the Duchesne River drainage, westward, over to the Provo River.

The Uintas are also a land of lakes, with more than 1,000 natural lakes residing within its borders. Some of the lakes have been dammed and expanded to increase water storage for the greater area.

The area boasts more than 500 miles of streams and receives an average of 40 inches of moisture annually.

In the summer, the Uintas are a popular recreation haven. State Highway 150 (also known as U-150 or the Mirror Lake Highway) is paved and traverses from the west side of the mountains to the northeast side. Hiking, backpacking, fishing, sightseeing, camping, and picnicking are all popular activities.

In the early fall, catching sight of the fall leaves is a regular attraction, and in winter, a more limited number of hardy souls cross-country ski, snowshoe, or snowmobile in the Uinta Mountains.

Mirror Lake is considered the centerpiece of camping in the Uintas and, in July, finding an open campsite there usually requires advance planning and reservations.

The Uintas are about 50 air miles from Salt Lake City, and the drive there—all on paved roads—requires little more than an hour to their border.

Temperatures above 10,000 feet rarely top 80 degrees Fahrenheit in summer, and they fall to the 30s and 40s or sometimes even lower on summer nights. The Uintas are the best place to escape scorching summer heat along the Wasatch Front. Getting wet by at least a few raindrops is more common than not on a typical summer afternoon.

The High Uintas are truly the "roof" of Utah, with elevations exceeding 13,000 feet above sea level. In fact, they are a rare east-west running mountain range and are the tallest such angled range in the lower 48 states. The Uintas also have more territory above timberline than any other mountain range in the continental United States.

The Uinta Mountains comprise more than 450,000 acres, with Kings Peak, 13,528 feet above sea level, as the range's and the state's tallest point. Most hikers begin an assault on Kings Peak from the north side, in Henry's Fork. From parking lot to summit is about a 15-mile, one-way trek. Most split it into a three-day or more backpacking trip, while others conquer it in one endurance-testing day hike.

In 1965, the US Forest Service reported that hikers to Kings Peak numbered less than 30 a year, and it was common to find solitude on the summit. By the 21st century, "peak bagging" fever had struck, and 50 or more hikers visiting Kings Peak each summer day was not uncommon.

The highest of Uinta peaks are littered with slabs of rock; the entire area experienced glaciers during the last ice age. Notwithstanding, because of lesser precipitation, the Uintas are the only mountain range above 13,000 feet in elevation that lacks glaciers in the nation. Much of the rock in the Uintas, mostly Precambrian, is more than 600 million years old.

There are more than 500 miles of trails in the Uintas, highlighted by the 104-mile-long Highline Trail that goes east and west through the middle of the range.

The range is 150 miles long and 30 miles wide.

Much of the Uintas was designated as a wilderness area in 1984, through the Utah Wilderness Act. (Notwithstanding, this law grandfathered some existing livestock uses, meaning you will still encounter cattle and sheep in portions of the wilderness area.)

Moose, elk, mule deer, mountain goats, back bears, bighorn sheep, cougars, river otters, and many other animals, plus dozens of different bird species, call the Uintas home.

Fish are plentiful in some of the lakes and are occasionally restocked by airplane drops.

Early summer wetlands can produce numerous biting mosquitoes that can plague hikers and backpackers. Repellents can be a "must take" accessory for visitors. Higher elevations can also feature pesky flies. Sturdy footwear is essential here, and blisters have plagued many hikers with poor or not broken-in footwear.

Motorized vehicles are not allowed in the wilderness area, and three roads—Murdock Basin, Broadhead Meadows, and East Portal—link some 20 miles of ATV (all-terrain vehicle) trails. Snowmobiling must be outside the wilderness area and be on existing roads and trails.

Despite its wilderness status, water should be filtered or purified in the Uintas before drinking.

The area's most dangerous natural hazards include lightning strikes from quick-moving storms, isolation that can turn a moderate medical emergency into a major one, and high altitude that can lead to rapid dehydration and/or altitude sickness. Sudden storms can also increase dangers from hypothermia. Sunscreen and hats are suggested too, especially given the high-intensity sunlight at the Uintas's extreme altitudes.

Approaching a moose with a calf may be the most dangerous wildlife threat here. Some rattlesnakes exist on the lower elevation outskirts of the Uintas but are unable to survive at the main elevations.

The High Uintas was also home to the highest elevation Boy Scout camp in the nation for decades. Located less than four miles from Mirror Lake is Camp Steiner (now not a scout camp, but a high adventure base camp) at 10,400 feet above sea level (and adjacent to Scout Lake). There are also a few other scout camps in the Uintas.

The High Uintas are also a key source of legends and folktales. Spanish gold is rumored to be buried somewhere in the Uinta Mountains.

The first ever widespread sighting of Bigfoot in Utah was also in the High Uintas, on August 22, 1977. Two men and six teenagers from North Ogden City claimed they saw a gorilla-like creature who matched the description of a bigfoot.

The famous Skinwalker Ranch, a hotbed for unexplained phenomenon, is located just southwest of Fort Duchesne, in the Uinta Basin, below the southeast edge of the Uinta Mountains.

One

EARLY EXPLORATION

The Ute Indians likely hunted and fished in the Uintas whenever the warmer seasons of the year permitted. But living there year-round was too inhospitable.

The Utes were hunters and gatherers. Their contact with the Spanish provided them with horses and greater mobility. Then, when the Mormon settlers arrived, conflicts arose. The Spanish Fork Treaty was signed by the Utes in 1865. They were forced to move into the dry portion of the Uintah Basin. By 1881, the Ouray Reservation was formed, but more than 90 percent of their land was eventually taken away by the government. (The Utes received $32 million during the 1950s in reparations for these land losses.)

The Spanish expedition from Santa Fe in 1776, headed by Francisco Atanasio Dominguez and Silvestre Velez de Escalante, likely included the first white men to see the Uinta Mountains.

Following the greater leadership stability after the end of the Civil War, the US government sponsored three geological expeditions west of the 100th meridian. One survey was by John Wesley Powell, another by Clarence King, and the third by Ferdinand V. Hayden. All three surveys overlapped in the Uinta Mountains, and these men named many features, took photographs, and outlined this wilderness area.

Wesley Powell entered the Uintas first in the fall of 1868. (He returned to the Uintas in 1874–1875 to complete his research.) At the start of Powell's trip, Uinta was originally spelled "Uintah," but Powell dropped the "h" as being redundant.

In 1869, Powell wrote about the Uintas: "Away to the south, the Uinta Mountains stretch in a long line; high peaks thrust(ing) into the sky, and snowfields glittering like lakes of molten silver; and pine forests in somber green; and rosy clouds playing around the borders of huge, black masses."

Clarence King's exploration of the Uintas was in the summers of 1869 and 1871 for his Fortieth Parallel Survey. Kings Peak is named in his honor.

Ferdinand V. Hayden explored the Uintas in 1870. Hayden Peak, 12,479 feet above sea level in the Uintas, is named after him.

Pictured here in 1902 is a typical Ute family living in western Colorado, just east of the Uinta Mountains. In their pre-reservation days, the Utes would only hunt and fish in the Uintas during the warmer months of the year, since the harsh winters there prevented year-round settlements. (Courtesy of Library of Congress.)

Five Ute women are shown in an 1899 photograph. The Utes were traditionally hunters and gatherers, but the arrival of white settlers competed for their resources and land. The Utes had obtained their first horses when the Spanish came through their area around 1680. (Courtesy of Library of Congress.)

Pictured here are Clarence King (right side) and his US government field crew of 1864, when they were appointed to survey the boundary of Yosemite Valley. Their mission was appointed by Pres. Abraham Lincoln. Three years later, in 1867, King was assigned to conduct the Fortieth Parallel Survey, which included the Uinta Mountains. (Courtesy of Smithsonian National Portrait Gallery.)

The Clarence King camp, near Salt Lake City, is shown in October 1868, in between expeditions to the Uinta Mountains as part of the Fortieth Parallel Survey. A year later, King would be appointed the first director of the newly created US Geological Survey. (Courtesy of Library of Congress.)

An 1868 or 1869 photograph shows a lake near the headwaters of the Bear River in the Uinta Mountains at an elevation of nearly 11,000 feet above sea level. The lake is possibly Norice Lake or Priord Lake but was originally known as Moores Lake. The picture was taken by Andrew Joseph Russell. (Courtesy of Library of Congress.)

This is an 1869 photograph from the Fortieth Parallel Survey, near the headwaters of the Bear River. It is on this lofty plateau where the river begins a nearly 500-mile-long journey through three states—Utah, Wyoming, and Idaho—on the way to the Great Salt Lake. (Courtesy of Library of Congress.)

This is another photograph from the government expeditions in 1869, taken near the headwaters of the Bear River. This is likely Yard Peak, a 12,706-foot elevation summit that is known for its rugged nature. Snow from this peak feeds the Bear River headwaters. (Courtesy of Library of Congress.)

This picture from 1869 was taken as part of the Fortieth Parallel Survey by Clarence King in the vicinity of the headwaters of the Bear River. Surveyors wanted to trace the beginnings of the Bear River, since its waters are so vital to the region. Note the two Native Americans, possibly Utes, in the lower right-hand side of the picture. (Courtesy of Library of Congress.)

Agassiz Peak is shown in an 1869 photograph. At 12,428 feet above sea level, the peak was named in honor of Louis Agassiz, a Swiss-born American geologist and botanist. Although there is no defined trail to its summit, the peak is often climbed due to its accessibility. It is one of the easiest summits to climb above 12,000 feet. (Courtesy of Library of Congress.)

Lake Lall (or Lal as it was sometimes written) is shown in an 1869 photograph from the US government surveys in the Uinta Mountains. The name *Lake Lall* did not stick, though, and today the lake is likely Ryder Lake or possibly Blue Lake. Agassiz Peak is nearby. (Courtesy of Library of Congress.)

This is another picture of Lake Lall, taken in 1869. Andrew J. Russell took this photograph as part of the US Geological Survey of the Fortieth Parallel. Note the extremely rocky terrain amidst all the surrounding trees. (Courtesy of Library of Congress.)

Another 1869 US government photograph shows Agassiz Peak and either Ryder Lake or Blue Lake. There is no trail to the Agassiz summit, but an approximate seven-mile, round-trip hike is the shortest path from U-150. Spread Eagle Peak is found just east of Agassiz Peak, and Hayden Peak sits to the north. (Courtesy of Library of Congress.)

This early–US government picture from the High Uintas is titled "Castle Lake;" however, no lake can be spotted in the photograph. (Perhaps it is in the far distance underneath the rugged peak shown.) There are two men visible in this stereographic picture at right center. Today, no lake is known as Castle Lake. Could this be a reference to today's Red Castle Lake? (Courtesy of New York Public Library.)

A stereographic view of Gilbert Peak is shown in 1870. This image is from a US government expedition, and it is likely a surveyor shown sitting down beside the lake. Gilbert Peak is the second-highest peak in the Uintas and in Utah at 13,448 feet above sea level. The lake shown is possibly Henry's Fork Lake. (Courtesy of New York Public Library.)

This stereographic view, taken by Andrew Joseph Russell between 1868 and 1870 in the Uinta Mountains for a US government survey, shows Shadow Lake. The picture is titled "Rocky Mountain Scenery." Note the thick vegetation in the picture. (Courtesy of Library of Congress.)

Here, Shadow Lake can be seen in the distance. Shadow Lake is an important part of the Provo River drainage. The lake is up to 17 feet deep and covers 18 acres at an elevation of 9,900 feet above sea level. (Courtesy of Library of Congress.)

Shadow Lake is pictured here around 1870. Note the many large rock formations sitting around the lake and the government surveyor atop one of them, admiring the scenery. The lake's name may come from the late afternoon shadows over the water, caused by a nearby mountain located to the west that blocks the sun. (Courtesy of Library of Congress.)

A summer of 1870 stereographic photograph from US government photographer Andrew Joseph Russell shows water leaving Shadow Lake and entering the Provo River drainage. The picture also illustrates just how rugged the High Uintas landscape can be, with countless large boulders and numerous lofty peaks. (Courtesy of Library of Congress.)

Flaming Gorge is shown in this 1872 photograph from the US Geological Survey of the Fortieth Parallel, led by Clarence King. This gorge is located along the Green River in the extreme northeast corner of the Uinta Mountains. The picture was taken by Timothy H. O'Sullivan. (Courtesy of Library of Congress.)

20

This is an 1872 picture of Garnet Canyon in the Uinta Mountains. Once again, this early place name did not duplicate beyond the original US government survey of northeastern Utah Territory. So, though it appears to be in the lower elevations of the Uintas, it is uncertain exactly where it is today. (Courtesy of Library of Congress.)

Shown in this 1870 photograph is what early surveyors proclaimed as a "miniature" El Capitan in the Uinta Mountains. Taken by William Henry Jackson, this image shows that the peak does resemble the famous Yosemite cliff, though this version seems flatter on top. Where this mini El Capitan is specifically located was not specified, but the same government explorers had surveyed in Yosemite just a few years prior. (Courtesy of National Archives.)

This government survey photograph from 1870 shows a distant view of the snow-covered Uinta Mountains. The location of the picture is the foothills bordering the Bear River, which puts this near or even over the Wyoming border. Given that there is still snow in the Uintas, the time of year is likely late springtime, when surveyors could not yet easily travel into the high elevations. (Courtesy of Library of Congress.)

Two

LOFTY ROAD BUILDING

The first road in the Uintas actually traversed north and south. The Carter Road was built in 1881 by the US Army because of Ute Indian raids. The road was previously a Ute trail. It went from Fort Bridger, Wyoming, south to Fort Thornburgh (northwest of Vernal). Only a few sections of it are in use today.

Going from west to east, first there was a horse path from Kamas to Mirror Lake. Then, it became a wagon trail by the 1880s. The Civilian Conservation Corps (CCC) greatly improved that wagon path in the High Uintas, from Soapstone to Mirror Lake, in the early 1930s.

The road was originally called Provo River Road or the Provo River-Hayden's Fork Road.

Perhaps the first report of automobile travel on that route was in the late summer of 1930, when regional forester R.H. Rutledge went by auto from Ogden to Mirror Lake before starting an eight-day horse trip that traversed through some 300,000 acres of wilderness. It was advertised as amazing that the road only had a maximum grade of eight percent.

In 1935, the dirt road through the High Uintas was still very limited. This dirt road was improved in 1937–1938, and summer motorists could now drive from Kamas to Mirror Lake in just two hours. But there was a strong desire by Utah and Wyoming officials to make it a through road, past Mirror Lake and all the way to Evanston, Wyoming. This road punched through in the summer of 1940. The extra 9.5 miles past Mirror Lake connected with Highway 30 out of Evanston. A CCC work crew of 125 men and heavy equipment were required.

World War II then delayed any further improvements. By 1960, the highway's final seven miles were paved from Mirror Lake to Evanston and eventually designated Highway 150 and a scenic route. Mirror Lake Highway (U-150) is 42 miles long and crosses Bald Mountain Pass, 10,759 feet above sea level, and is the highest paved road in Utah. The road is usually open June to early November, depending on the weather. Its latest-ever opening was June 29, 1995.

The Carter Road was the first wagon trail, from north to south, in the Uinta Mountains. Indian trouble led to its creation in the 1880s, though parts of it had been used as early as 1865. The rugged road went from Fort Bridger, south into the Uinta Basin, and ended at Fort Thornburgh, near Vernal. When Fort Thornburgh was abandoned in 1884, residents of Daggett County used the road until 1924, when other, better routes became available. (Courtesy of Utah State Historical Society.)

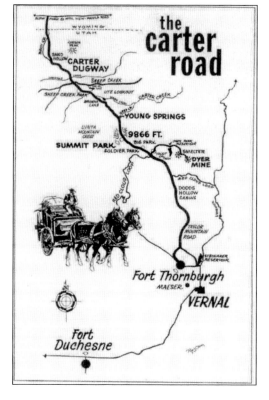

Shown is a map of the Carter Road through the Uinta Mountains. When the route's military purpose vanished, it became heavily used to access the Dyer Mine, a copper mine that also yielded gold and silver. Today, signs of the old, historic road are still visible. (Courtesy of Utah State Historical Society.)

This picture shows what the road to Mirror Lake looked like in the 1930s. It was a narrow, dirt path, with hardly room for any passing. This section appears to be coming off Bald Mountain Pass and descending east toward Mirror Lake. The first reports of automobiles reaching the lake were in the summer of 1930. (Courtesy of Utah State Historical Society.)

This is another view of the Mirror Lake road as it descends off the Bald Mountain summit (elevation 10,759 feet) and drops over 250 feet to the lake. Mirror Lake has always been the most popular lake in this section of the Uintas. The entire road, from Kamas to Evanston, was not paved until 1960. (Courtesy of J. Willard Marriott Digital Library, the University of Utah.)

This photograph from the summer of 1933 shows a Civilian Conservation Corps work camp in the High Uintas. CCC work crews built many roads and trails in the nation during the Great Depression. Here, the CCC widened and improved the road to Mirror Lake, making it faster and easier for automobile travel. (Courtesy of Utah State Historical Society.)

The CCC work camp at Mirror Lake is shown here, possibly during the mid-1930s. CCC jobs gave critical employment to out-of-work men during the Great Depression. The CCC also performed labors vital to road and trail building in remote locations, like the High Uintas. (Courtesy of Utah State Historical Society and the Delta, Utah Library.)

This picture shows a summer automobile excursion to the High Uintas. Ray King, resting on his car's front bumper, is shown with a group of friends and possibly family on a day trip to Mirror Lake. King was a photographer for the *Salt Lake Tribune* for many years and also used pictures to chronicle his personal life. (Courtesy of Utah State Historical Society.)

The western side of the Mirror Lake Highway as it appeared in the 1930s is shown here. The road, originating on the east side of Kamas, was often muddy and open only for the peak summer season. Still, the rugged road accessed a scenic wonderland for Utahns. (Courtesy of Utah State Historical Society.)

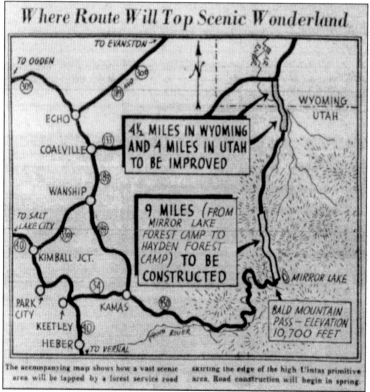

A map from the February 4, 1940, issue of the *Salt Lake Tribune* outlines upcoming summer plans for road work along the highway to Mirror Lake. This road punched through past the lake in the summer of 1940. The extra 9.5 miles past Mirror Lake connected with Highway 30 out of Evanston. A CCC work crew of 125 men and heavy equipment were required for the project. (Courtesy of *Salt Lake Tribune* Photo Archives.)

Three

THE ROOF OF UTAH

The Uintas are the "Alps" of Utah and yet their high elevations do not come without a cost.

For example, in 1937, a tragedy prompted United Airlines to increase its flight levels over northern Utah from 13,000 to 14,000 feet to make sure airplanes cleared the Uinta Mountains. This decision came a few weeks after a plane crashed into a 10,000-foot elevation mountain in the Uintas and killed 19 people.

A helicopter crashed on South Kings Peak on June 16, 1961. The crew was able to walk away and eventually met a rescue party. The helicopter was repaired, and all traces of it were removed from the mountain. (Flying helicopters in such high elevations are extra dangerous given the less air density.)

Kings Peak, the state's highest mountain, was actually unknown until 1966, when new survey methods "discovered" it. Previously, today's South Kings Peak, at a 13,512-foot elevation, was thought to be the tallest. Located less than a mile northwest of South Kings Peak, the current Kings Peak was measured to be 13,528 feet above sea level. At the same time, South Kings's elevation was revised from 13,498 feet to 13,512. Any hikers before 1966 who wanted to ascend the state's highest peak mistakenly bypassed the true highest "King" to an actual shorter summit.

The 10 tallest named peaks in the Uintas are 1) Kings Peak, Duchesne County, 13,528; 2) South Kings Peak, Duchesne County, 13,512; 3) Gilbert Peak, Summit and Duchesne Counties, 13,442; 4) Mount Emmons, Duchesne County, 13,440; 5) Mount Lovenia, Summit and Duchesne Counties; 13,219; 6) Tokewanna Peak, Summit County, 13,165; 7) Mount Powell, Summit County, 13,159; 8) Wasatch Peak, benchmark, Summit County, 13,156; 9) Wilson Peak, Summit and Duchesne Counties, 13,049; and 10) Squaw Peak, benchmark, Summit County, 12,990. (Note that there are still at least 14 unnamed peaks over 13,000 feet above sea level in the Uinta Mountains.) The highest Utah mountain outside the Uintas is Mount Peale in the La Sal Mountains in San Juan County at 12,721 feet.

This 1880s US government photograph shows the east side of Bald Mountain, with Mirror Lake looming below. Bald Mountain is Utah's most easily climbed nearly 12,000-foot summit, since it sits along the highway to Mirror Lake—and only requires about a 1,200-foot rise to reach its peak. (Courtesy of the Brigham Young University Lee Library.)

This is an undated picture of the Bald Mountain summit, possibly from the 1920s, showing a man surveying the ground below through binoculars. The mountain is so named because it is almost entirely devoid of vegetation. The mountain's only significant plants reside mostly on its western flank. (Courtesy of Utah State Historical Society.)

The four Chain Lakes, located in the Krebs Basin, are shown in this undated picture, possibly from the 1940s. Accessing these lakes is a rugged 24-mile, round-trip backpacking adventure, with some 3,000 feet in elevation gain required. However, the long distance and climb equal an uncrowded experience in a less often visited portion of the High Uintas. (Courtesy of Utah State Historical Society.)

This 1930 view from the Wasatch Mountain Club's collection is looking from a northeast direction toward Bald Mountain. The larger lake in the photograph is Mirror Lake, while the smaller is Pass Lake. The picture was likely taken from along today's Lofty Lake Trail. (Courtesy of J. Willard Marriott Digital Library, the University of Utah.)

Granddaddy Lake is one of the largest bodies of water in the High Uintas at 170 acres in size. It is a popular hiking and backpacking destination from July to September, on a 16-mile-long loop. Horses also share the same trail in this wilderness area. (Courtesy of Utah State Historical Society.)

This undated photograph may be from the 1930s and shows Reid's Peak, a prominent, stand-alone peak just northeast of Bald Mountain. Reid's Peak is 11,572 feet above sea level, or about 350 feet shorter than Bald Mountain. Reid's Peak was named for a trapper who came through the area around 1875. (Courtesy of Utah State Historical Society.)

Lamotte Peak is shown in this photograph from the 1930s. While the elevation on the picture states an elevation of 12,750 feet, modern measurements have lowered that to 12,720, making Lamotte the 94th tallest summit in the state of Utah. (Courtesy of J. Willard Marriott Digital Library, the University of Utah.)

William H. Hopkins (1873–1958), a member of the Wasatch Mountain Club, stands atop West Granddaddy peak in the Uinta Mountains, in the early 1920s. Granddaddy Lake occupies the valley below. Hopkins was also a Salt Lake City dentist, photographer, and tourism promoter. (Courtesy of J. Willard Marriott Digital Library, the University of Utah.)

Fifteen members of the Wasatch Mountain Club (including four women) pose for a picture in the High Uintas before embarking on hikes to the top of Mount Hayden and also Agassiz Peak, probably in the early 1930s. (Note that two club members are wearing shorts.) Homer A. Collins likely took the picture. The two peaks are less than two miles apart but would have required separate climbs/descents, as no ridge connects the two summits. (Courtesy of J. Willard Marriott Digital Library, the University of Utah.)

This undated photograph, likely from the 1930s, highlights the large crack in a mountain ridge in the High Uintas. Although no glaciers exist in the Uintas today, in prehistoric times, they existed there and sculpted a lot of the rugged peaks and valleys in the area. (Courtesy of J. Willard Marriott Digital Library, the University of Utah.)

A lone horse stands on Red Knob Pass in the High Uintas during a pack trip from August 1 to August 12, 1930. Two doctors, Dr. William H. Hopkins and Dr. L.D. Pfouts, were on this outdoor trip. Red Knob Pass is just over 12,000 feet above sea level, and even with today's trails, it would have required a jaunt of more than eight miles to access it from any road. (Courtesy of J. Willard Marriott Digital Library, the University of Utah.)

The August 1930 trip by Dr. William H. Hopkins and Dr. L.D. Pfouts included a visit to Tiger Head Lake. Three horses pasture around the lake, while a stationary camera is being set up. Many lakes in the High Uintas are still unnamed, and no modern mention of Tiger Head Lake could be found. Perhaps it was a nickname for a lake nearly a century ago? (Courtesy of J. Willard Marriott Digital Library, the University of Utah.)

Some three dozen employees of the US Forest Service in Utah pose at a conference in February 1923 at the Hotel Roberts in Provo. These employees were essential to the early management of the High Uintas. Note that this historic hotel opened in 1882 but was demolished in 2004. (Courtesy of Utah State Historical Society.)

A fleet of 45 new US Forest Service rangers from all over the intermountain area pose during a five-week training session in September and October 1945. Held at an old CCC work camp, near Tony Grove in Logan Canyon, the event was designed to provide field training for young rangers, including those that worked in the Uinta Mountains. (Courtesy of J. Willard Marriott Digital Library, the University of Utah.)

Dr. L.D. Pfouts travels across a snowfield on a horse pulling a packhorse during an August 1930 trip into the wilderness of the High Uintas. Snow can still linger into August at such high elevations. Pfouts was associated with the Wasatch Mountain Club and went to the Red Knob area on this trip. (Courtesy of J. Willard Marriott Digital Library, the University of Utah.)

Red Castle Peak is featured in this 1903 photograph. This peak is one of the most photographed in all of the Uinta Mountains, especially when the afternoon sun lights it up. Rising to an elevation of 12,566 feet, the shortest hike to Red Castle is about 10 miles, one-way, with an elevation gain of 1,400 feet. (Courtesy of Utah State Historical Society.)

A member of the Wasatch Mountain Club captured this panoramic picture of the High Uintas in the summer of 1930. Note the lingering snow on the slopes of some of the lofty peaks. Snow can fall during any month of the year in the Uinta Mountains. (Courtesy of J. Willard Marriott Digital Library, the University of Utah.)

A fisherman, who has already caught several fish, fishes for more near an unidentified 10-foot waterfall in the Uinta Mountains, probably in the 1940s. There are hundreds of miles of rapid, turbulent streams in the Uintas as well as more than 1,000 lakes. (Courtesy of Utah State Historical Society.)

This is a panoramic photograph from the 1940s or 1950s showing a large, forested section of the High Uintas. Portions of the Uintas are well above timberline, but there are significant sections with trees, including lodgepole pine, Douglas fir, Engelmann spruce, quaking aspen, and other varieties. (Courtesy of Utah State Historical Society.)

This is a 1941 photograph showing cattle grazing on the outskirts of the Uinta Mountains, probably in springtime. This picture, taken in the Heber City area, was shot by Russell Lee. There are many farming and ranching operations near the Uintas, since they usually have moderate temperatures and adequate moisture. (Courtesy of New York Public Library.)

This is another 1941 photograph in the Heber City area showing the snow-covered Uinta Mountains. The picture, taken by Russell Lee, shows a large field of dandelions in front of telephone wires and some farms in the distance. (Courtesy of New York Public Library.)

Sir Edmund Hillary, one of two men to first climb to the summit of Mount Everest in 1953, visited, camped, and hiked in the High Uintas twice, first in 1962 and again in 1978. He did not care for the mosquitoes but enjoyed the lakes and the spectacular mountain scenery, like that shown here in Henry's Fork Basin. (Photograph by Ravell Call.)

Erma Hiatt is shown apparently shaving the face of an unidentified man at a campground, possibly near Mirror Lake, in the High Uintas during August 1930. Note the established picnic table in the picture. The Uintas were a summer favorite of Utahns, especially because temperatures there could be 25 degrees Fahrenheit or cooler than the Wasatch Front in a typical July or August. (Courtesy of J. Willard Marriott Digital Library, the University of Utah.)

Seven unidentified leaders from the Boy Scouts of America, likely from the Great Salt Lake Council, pose in front of a High Uintas cabin, probably in the 1940s. The cabin could be at Camp Steiner, an actual Boy Scout Camp, or it could be at Mirror Lake, just a few miles away. Camp Steiner was once the highest-elevation Boy Scout camp in the nation. Now the camp is a High Adventure Base Camp. (Courtesy of Utah State Historical Society.)

Four

CENTERPIECE, MIRROR LAKE

Mirror Lake is Utah's equivalent of Wyoming's Jenny Lake, next to the Teton Mountains. It offers a photogenic, peaceful retreat below the rugged-looking Bald Mountain.

The only Mirror Lake that the vast majority of Utahns knew until around 1930 was Yosemite's same-named lake. Surprisingly, it was the sport of fishing that seemed to spur road building to Utah's lesser-known Mirror Lake; fish have been regularly stocked in the lake since the 1930s.

By 1925, the road reached Trial Lake, which is 25 miles east of Kamas but still seven miles short of Mirror Lake. Ever since, automobile travel in the summer was available by a narrow, dirt road. Starting around 1927, Utahns have been camping and fishing at Mirror Lake.

There are about 78 prized camping spots at Mirror Lake, and reservations are a must. In years with low snowfall, they may be open as early as the Fourth of July, but sometimes it is several weeks later.

Mirror Lake used to have a lodge and offer overnight accommodations. It opened in 1933 and boasted a café, service station, store, and cabins. In 1952, the US Forest Service took over operation of the lodge. The lodge was closed and completely removed a few years later, likely due to the extremely short season of use there.

Within a radius of just six miles, there are an additional 78 smaller lakes. Just southeast of Mirror Lake, in the Granddaddy Basin, are another 350 lakes. Foot trails lead from Mirror Lake into these nearby basins.

The water that replenishes Mirror Lake is overflow from Pass Lake, located to the northeast. Outflow from Mirror Lake comprises the headwaters of the Duchesne River.

Campers boat and fish at Mirror Lake or just lounge around and escape the summer heat of the Wasatch Front. Others just make a day drive to the lake and picnic.

The lake's name comes from how sharply it can reflect the sky and adjacent Bald Mountain on its surface waters.

Mirror Lake encompasses 50 acres, has a maximum depth of 41 feet, and an average depth of 17 feet. At least one person has died in the lake; in August 1934, a 19-year-old Bountiful man drowned there.

This 1940s picture shows two young men fishing along the shores of Mirror Lake, with Bald Mountain looming in the background. Mirror Lake is the namesake of the nearby paved scenic highway. The lake is so named because of its tranquil waters and reflections of the surrounding mountainous alpine setting. (Courtesy of Utah State Historical Society.)

The campsite of Dr. L.D. Pfouts and some friends at Mirror Lake in the summer of 1929 is shown here. Even before there was a smooth road here, the Pfouts and others would relax annually at the lake. This picture was taken by Dr. William H. Hopkins, a friend of Dr. Pfouts. (Courtesy of J. Willard Marriott Digital Library, the University of Utah.)

Mirror Lake was a bustling mountain campground even as early as the 1930s, as this historic photograph proves. From campfires to fishing and relaxation, this is still perhaps the most popular lake in all of the Uinta Mountains. Mirror Lake is located 32 miles east of Kamas and has more than 70 designated camping sites. (Courtesy of Utah State Historical Society.)

Sometime in the 1930s, Ray King and his companion showcase their large catch of a dozen or more fish at Mirror Lake from atop their small boat. King was a frequent visitor to Mirror Lake. This 50-acre lake sits at 10,500 feet above sea level and is regularly stocked with trout, usually rainbow and Eastern brook. (Courtesy of Utah State Historical Society.)

Ray King (standing) frolics with three friends, (from left to right) June, Betty, and Dick, on the shores of Mirror Lake in the summer of 1943. Back in this era, there was an established lodge at Mirror Lake, and boats could be rented there. Mirror Lake is up to 41 feet deep, though the average depth is 17 feet. (Courtesy of Utah State Historical Society.)

Ray King and his friends (from left to right) June, Betty, and Dick are shown apparently eating Chinese food at Mirror Lake in the summer of 1943. King was a photographer for the *Salt Lake Tribune*, and this picture is part of his extensive photo collection. (Courtesy of Utah State Historical Society.)

A teenage woman and a young boy fish from a small boat at Mirror Lake during the 1940s. Today, the campground around Mirror Lake offers dozens of campsites, with picnic tables, tent pads, campfire rings, and grills. There are even 14 equestrian sites available. There are also pit toilets around Mirror Lake. (Courtesy of Utah State Historical Society.)

Mirror Lake is shown in this 1930s picture. In that era, Mann's Mirror Lake Lodge operated from 1933 to the early 1960s every summer. James and Mae "Peggy" Mann operated this lodge next to Mirror Lake for many years. It was eventually sold and became the Mirror Lake Lodge, featuring cabin rentals, boating, and horse trips. (Courtesy of Utah State Historical Society.)

This is a view of Mirror Lake on August 1, 1929, another vintage photograph from the Wasatch Mountain Club's collection. At that time, with increasing usage of automobiles and a better dirt road to access the area, Mirror Lake was taking off in popularity. Since that time, it has always been the most favored Uinta Mountains destination. (Courtesy of J. Willard Marriott Digital Library, the University of Utah.)

Five

LAND OF A
1,000-PLUS LAKES

The Uinta Mountains are a land of lakes. There are more than 1,000 natural lakes and ponds in the area. Some have been enlarged and dammed. At least half, about 500, support fish. Because there are so many lakes, a duplication of names exists. Some 17 lake names were misspelled or misnamed over the decades, but popular usage has overruled historical accuracy.

The top of Bald Mountain, near the Mirror Lake Highway, is perhaps the best spot in the Uintas to view numerous lakes. More than 70 lakes are visible from the summit, 11,928 feet above sea level.

Some of the most popular lakes are found along the paved Mirror Lake Highway, with sometimes a walk of less than 100 feet. These include Mirror Lake, Trial Lake, Lilly Lake, Washington Lake, Teapot Lake, Ruth Lake, Lost Lake, Moosehorn Lake, Pass Lake, and Butterfly Lake.

Moon Lake, on the Uinta's south side, is a large, popular lake accessible by car. Foot and horse trails from there access Brown Duck Lake, Kidney Lake, and Island Lake.

Before the days of fish stocking by airplanes, the first big account to planting fish was reported in August 1928, when a large bus and several automobiles carried some 80,000 fish to the Uintas. These trout were planted at Mirror Lake and some nearby lakes.

One of the deepest lakes is Wall Lake. Actually a reservoir with a dam, the natural lake was expanded. It can have a maximum depth of 128 feet and an average depth of 31 feet. However, it can fluctuate some 40 feet lower, depending on climate and outflow. Upper Red Castle Lake is one of the deepest natural lakes, dipping down 105 feet.

Cliff Lake, near Kings Peak, is one of the highest elevation of lakes in the Uintas, at 11,600 feet.

Forest fires are a large potential hazard in the Uintas, despite the presence of so many lakes and streams. For example, on June 28, 2002, Boy Scouts may have started the East Fork of the Bear River Fire that burned some 14,000 acres in the Uintas.

This is Flaming Gorge as shown in an 1872 US government photograph. The gorge has always been known for its spectacular red walls and its very arid, green forest. When this picture was taken, there was no dam on the Green River. Today, there is a 91-mile-long reservoir, spanning Wyoming and Utah. (Courtesy of Library of Congress.)

A family of seven enjoys Lily Pad Lake (Duchesne County) during a 1937 summer outing. There are seven other lakes in the Uintas that use the name "Lily" in their title, including another identically named lake in Summit County. The lily pads that usually adorn the surface of the lake are likely the namesake of all similar bodies of water. (Courtesy of J. Willard Marriott Digital Library, the University of Utah.)

The Weber River is shown, not far from the Smith and Morehouse Reservoir, near the western edge of the Uinta Mountains. The Weber is one of four major rivers with headwaters in the Uintas. The Weber River is also the major water supplier for both the Rockport and Echo Reservoirs, downstream. (Courtesy of Utah State Historical Society.)

The Provo River, in the Heber Valley, is pictured here in the early 1960s. Mount Timpanogos can be seen in the background. This river, with Uinta Mountain headwaters, has long been a favorite for fishermen in both Wasatch and Utah Counties. The Provo River also feeds into the Jordanelle and Deer Creek Reservoirs. (Courtesy of Utah State Historical Society.)

"FOUR LAKES" OF MORE THAN A THOUSAND IN THE UINTA MOUNTAINS

A postcard, possibly from the 1950s or 1960s, highlights four lakes in the Uintas, out of the 1,000-plus lakes that exist there. Some of the lakes there today are still not officially named. At least half of those lakes support a population of fish. (Used by permission, Uintah County Library Regional History Center, all rights reserved.)

This 1940s photograph clearly shows the Chain Lakes of the Uintas. They are so named because they are arranged like links of a chain. The four lakes are called Lower Lake, Middle Lake, Upper Lake, and Fourth Lake. They are located in the center of the High Uintas. (Courtesy of Utah State Historical Society.)

Another 1940s photograph shows one of the Chain Lakes close-up. This lake is located about three miles east of Mount Emmons, the fourth-highest peak in the Uintas. The Chain Lakes are located more than 11 miles from the nearest road. A couple of women on horseback are overlooking the lake. (Courtesy of Utah State Historical Society.)

Three men on horseback, plus a lone horse, are shown leaving the basin that contains the Chain Lakes in the summer of 1931. Since the group does not seem to be carrying many provisions, they may have been on a day's outing from a camp found elsewhere in the Uintas. The lone horse may be the animal of the photographer. (Courtesy of Utah State Historical Society.)

Two men enjoy the view at one of the Chain Lakes in an undated photograph, possibly from the 1940s. These four lakes are sometimes just numbered, No. 1 through No. 4. Chain Lake No. 3 is up to 65 feet deep. All the lakes sit at a 10,000-foot elevation. (Courtesy of Utah State Historical Society.)

King's Peak, the state's highest point, is reflected in a small, unnamed lake that sits near Anderson Pass, at the upper end of Henry's Fork. This undated picture may be from the early 1960s, when South Kings Peak (not shown, being behind Kings Peak) was still wrongly believed to be the state's highest point, which changed in 1966. (Courtesy of Utah State Historical Society.)

This is Moon Lake in August 1941. Located 25 miles north of Duchesne, on the southern end of the Uintas, it is a hub for boating, hiking, fishing, and camping. There is a campground as well as the Moon Lake Resort with cabins. Among other legends, there is a lake monster reputed to live in its waters sometimes called "Moonie," akin to the Loch Ness Monster. The area also has a number of ghost legends too. (Used by permission, Uintah County Library Regional History Center, all rights reserved.)

Six

MOUNTAINOUS INDUSTRIES

When driving along the Mirror Lake Highway (U-150), it is hard not to look upward at the majestic Uinta Mountain range. However, below the highway level is a feature just off the highway that most travelers miss. The concrete-lined Duchesne Tunnel is a $9 million, six-mile-long engineering marvel that is a key to providing water to Utah and Salt Lake Counties.

The tunnel takes water from the south slope of the Uinta Mountains in the Duchesne River drainage and moves it westward over the mountains to the Provo River drainage and into Deer Creek Reservoir.

This tunnel took 13.5 years to build and was completed on October 14, 1953. In a state as dry as Utah, water is likely the greatest overall natural resource that the Uintas provide.

Although the Uinta Mountain forest is not nearly as dense as Pacific Northwest forests, harvesting timber for wood construction has been a modest industry in the Uintas.

It was in 1911 that the US Forest Service first went into the Uinta Mountains and estimated how much timber there was and made plans for its commercial usage. The Standard Timber Company started timber harvesting in the fall of 1912, on the Mill Fork of the Bear River. Later, the company moved to the Middle Fork of the Bear River.

Livestock usage was a grandfathered in, allowing ranching use to continue in the Uintas after it was made a wilderness area. In summer, cattle and sheep graze in portions of the mountains. Large sheep herds have even been seen grazing in the upper Henry's Fork Basin, just north of Kings Peak.

There has also been occasional mining in the Uintas, but the mountains are perhaps best known—regarding mining—for the hoax perpetuated there. In 1871, diamonds were scattered in the Uintas and other places in the West to "salt the ground" and lure investors into a false mining prospect. Shortly thereafter, though, US geologist Clarence King helped survey the High Uintas. He was able to conclude that such diamonds were planted there and had potential investors notified before they lost all their money.

Some movies have also been filmed in the Uintas, like *Jeremiah Johnson* in 1972.

This was one of the earliest sawmills in the Uinta Mountains. In 1870, Judge W.A. Carter owned this mill. It was located about 22 miles south of Fort Bridger, Wyoming. Here, workers appear to be taking a rest break. (Courtesy of the Brigham Young University Lee Library, L. Tom Perry Special Collection.)

The Upper Provo Falls was roaring with water in this August 1930 picture. Coming from the High Uinta Mountains, this water along the upper Provo River has always been a prized resource to the many valleys and communities below. (Courtesy of J. Willard Marriott Digital Library, the University of Utah.)

This 1908 photograph shows Uinta Mountain water flowing in the Duchesne Canal. Construction on the canal started in 1906, soon after the Ute Reservation was opened for outside homestead in 1905. Its waters were critical to all the farms and ranches that sprang up in the Uinta Basin, south of the Uinta Mountains. (Courtesy of Library of Congress.)

This is an undated but more modern view of a section of the Duchesne Canal, possibly in the 1960s. The original canal here was built by Thomas Rhoads, with a team of horses and help from other settlers. Its existence underscores the strong cooperation that early settlers had. (Courtesy of Library of Congress.)

Horse-powered travel was the best transportation method in the 19th century. This 1890 photograph shows a wagon pulled by a team of horses in Uintah County, at the south end of the Uinta Mountains. Six travelers are shown, and all are wearing heavy coats on what must have been a chilly day. (Courtesy of J. Willard Marriott Digital Library, the University of Utah.)

An unidentified woman stands next to a US Forest Service sign in the 1950s. Although the sign reads "Wasatch National Forest," it is actually all about the High Uintas area and was probably located near or in the town of Kamas. The sign also includes warnings about being atop peaks during thunderstorms and not to roll rocks off trails. (Courtesy of J. Willard Marriott Digital Library, the University of Utah.)

This undated photograph, possibly from the 1960s, shows a lone sheep rancher on horseback in the Blue Lake area of the High Uintas. The river shown could be the Duchesne River. Ranchers in the area today still use horses because motorized travel is prohibited in the wilderness portion of the Uinta Mountains. (Courtesy of Utah State Historical Society.)

The Deep Creek Ranch is shown on the southern end of the Uinta Mountains. This 1940s view is looking northward from the Uinta Basin. Such ranches rely on water from snowmelt in the Uinta Mountains. Today, the most famous Uinta Basin ranch, the Skinwalker Ranch, is located miles to the southeast of here. It is a hotbed of paranormal activity. (Used by permission, Uintah County Library Regional History Center, all rights reserved.)

An unidentified man stands next to a large boulder that is blocking road-building efforts on the southern side of the Uinta Mountains, probably in the 1940s. Many key roads in the Uintas were built or improved in the 1930s and 1940s. Such large boulders are a common feature in the geology of the Uintas. (Used by permission, Uintah County Library Regional History Center, all rights reserved.)

A sheep operation is pictured here, possibly in the 1950s, with the High Uintas as its range. Pioneers used the Uintas for summer cattle and sheep grazing, and this usage was even sometimes grandfathered into the modern wilderness area designations for the mountains. For example, hikers trekking to Kings Peak can sometimes hear sheep bellowing in the valleys below. (Courtesy of Utah State Historical Society.)

This is a fire training seminar on May 27, 1953, in the Whiterocks area, just south of the Uinta Mountains. About four dozen men participated in the training. Wildfires are a keen danger in the dry summer months in the Uinta Basin and can threaten not just farms, but nearby towns, like Neola and Roosevelt. (Used by permission, Uintah County Library Regional History Center, all rights reserved.)

Spirit Lake is shown in this undated photograph, possibly from the 1950s. This 53-acre lake, located on the east side of the Uinta Mountains, can be up to 28 feet deep. At 10,600 feet above sea level, it has a very short summer season. The Spirit Lake Lodge is also located near the lake. Like many High Uinta areas, there is sparse cell phone reception at the lake. (Used by permission, Uintah County Library Regional History Center, all rights reserved.)

This is an undated photograph of the Dyer Mine. It was located in the extreme northeast corner of the Uinta Mountains, near Dutch John. Dyer was established in 1887 and primarily mined copper and silver. It was situated at an elevation of 9,800 feet above sea level. (Used by permission, Uintah County Library Regional History Center, all rights reserved.)

Besides its wealth in natural resources and recreation, the High Uintas are also sometimes used in movie-making projects. This 1971 photograph shows Robert Redford starring in *Jeremiah Johnson*. Some of the filming on the production was done in Whiterocks Canyon, shown here. The canyon is on the south slope of the Uintas, northeast of Neola. (Used by permission, Uintah County Library Regional History Center, all rights reserved.)

Seven

RECREATION HEAVEN

The "heights and clouds, and mountains and . . . forests and rocklands are blended into one grand view," explorer John Wesley Powell noted in a diary entry in May 1869. And his Uintas description remains apt to this day.

Camp Steiner, in the High Uintas, is the highest-elevation Boy Scout camp in the United States, sitting at 10,400 feet above sea level. This camp dates back to 1930. Located around aptly named Scout Lake, this camp is also only a few miles away from Mirror Lake. (There are also some other Scout camps and adventure camps located in the Uinta Mountains.)

Not to be outdone by Kamas, Vernal heavily highlighted its easy access to the Uinta Mountains starting in the 1940s. "Vernal is gateway to scenic areas of high Uinta mountains" was a 1941 headline in the *Vernal Express* newspaper.

Boy Scouts have also always loved to conquer Kings Peak, the state's tallest point. As early as August 1936, some 400 older Scouts from Utah County hiked to Kings Peak, with some coming from all directions in the county.

Some visitors to the Uintas have just one thing on their mind—fishing. With some 500 lakes stocked with fish, the area is a haven for fishermen.

Ever since the automobile became popular in the 1920s and with the Uintas being so high in elevation, visitors from the Wasatch Front have come to the mountains to escape the summer heat.

Once the Mirror Lake Highway was completed in the 1930s, it became an annual outing for northern Utah families to spend a few days camping in the Uintas. Children could frolic in nearby piles of snow, and parents could fish the lakes or just relax. Many a summer campfire burned after dark in the Uintas.

Horse lovers would bring their animals to the Uintas and have a much easier time traversing between lakes and conducting long backpacking trips.

Winter enthusiasts would snowshoe the Uintas, mostly on the outskirts, where the snow was not as deep and accessibility was better. By the 1960s, snowmobiles were a favorite mode of transportation, and then ATVs became popular.

This 1910 photograph shows a group of tourists ready to take a tour of the High Uinta forest on horseback. Some of the women riders appear to be wearing dresses, and a few of the horses are carrying blankets. Horse trips in the Uintas seem to have been more popular a century ago than today. (Used by permission,)

Vera Winterode is shown traveling by horseback in the High Uintas, around Mirror Lake, during the summer of 1929. Her lack of provisions indicates that she is probably out for a short trip. William H. Hopkins, a member of the Wasatch Mountain Club, took this photograph. (Courtesy of J. Willard Marriott Digital Library, the University of Utah.)

A man stops by a trail marker post on top of Dead Horse Pass, with a 11,300-foot elevation, during an August 1930 equestrian trip. The picture was taken by William H. Hopkins and the location ironic, considering it shows three horses on a pass named for dead horses. But there is a lake by the same name in the immediate area too. Dr. L.D. Pfouts was also a member of this group. (Courtesy of J. Willard Marriott Digital Library, the University of Utah.)

This 1940s photograph shows two women and one man on horseback in the High Uintas. Note the packhorse carrying their supplies. Presumably, a second man is taking the photograph. The area appears to be northeast of Mirror Lake. Note that unlike most outdoor photographs in the 1930s and earlier where all people are wearing hats, no one in this group is. (Courtesy of Utah State Historical Society.)

Here, a woman stands in front of Mirror Lake in the summer of 1934. Note the small boat on the lake as well as several campsites in the background. This is another picture by Ray King, longtime photographer for the *Salt Lake Tribune*. King loved the Utah outdoors and especially Mirror Lake. (Courtesy of Utah State Historical Society.)

A woman climbs ropes along the side of Hayden Peak in the Uinta Mountains during the 1930s. This was part of a Wasatch Mountain Club outing. Today, Hayden Peak, with a 12,479-foot elevation, is rated as a Class 3 mountain climb with easy access. (Most other Uinta Mountains are rated more difficult at Class 2.) The picture was probably taken by Homer A. Collins. (Courtesy of J. Willard Marriott Digital Library, the University of Utah.)

Two hikers are shown on the east flank of Hayden Peak during a Wasatch Mountain Club adventure in July 1931. McPheters Lake is shown below, and the Stillwater Fork of the Bear River lies just beyond that. Hayden Peak has easy access off the east side of the Mirror Lake Highway. (Courtesy of J. Willard Marriott Digital Library, the University of Utah.)

Five members of the Wasatch Mountain Club, including three women, converse after hiking to the summit of Hayden Peak in July 1931. Ryder Lake is shown below, and today's Kletting Peak is in the distance. Kletting Peak was untitled when this picture was taken. It was not named until 1964, after Richard K.A. Kletting, architect of the Utah State Capitol and a conservationist. (Courtesy of J. Willard Marriott Digital Library, the University of Utah.)

The public and state leaders gather on June 27, 1964, for the naming ceremony of Kletting Peak, seen in the background. The peak was previously unnamed. The mountain was named for Richard K.A. Kletting, architect and conservationist. Kletting also designed the Utah State Capitol Building as well as the original Saltair Resort. (Courtesy of Utah State Historical Society.)

Five Wasatch Mountain Club members sit on a dizzying cliff during an outing in the 1930s. The mountain is likely Hayden Peak or possibly Mount Agassiz. The photographer, Homer A. Collins, was probably perched on another cliff himself to capture this image. (Courtesy of J. Willard Marriott Digital Library, the University of Utah.)

The summit of Hayden Peak was conquered by these five people during a summer hike in the 1930s. It apparently was not a cold day, as even at almost a 12,500 elevation, one of the men is shirtless. Also note the mailbox imbedded in the rock cairn. Homer A. Collins likely took this picture for the Wasatch Mountain Club. (Courtesy of J. Willard Marriott Digital Library, the University of Utah.)

Eighteen members of the Wasatch Mountain Peak strategically pose on one of the Uinta Mountain peaks during the 1930s. This is possibly Hayden Peak, so close to the Mirror Lake Highway that it was easily accessible for summer day hikes. (Courtesy of J. Willard Marriott Digital Library, the University of Utah.)

Ten hikers pose atop Tokewanna Peak during a summer outing in the High Uintas. At an elevation of 13,165 feet, it is one of the most remote peaks in the Uintas. In fact, it is the sixth-tallest summit in the state of Utah. To access the peak requires a challenging 21-mile round-trip hike. (Courtesy of J. Willard Marriott Digital Library, the University of Utah.)

Camping in the High Uintas 1920s style, three unidentified men break camp. One man is checking his horse's hoofs and filing off rough spots. Another is filling the saddle packs, and the third man is working with another piece of equipment. (Used by permission, Uintah County Library Regional History Center, all rights reserved.)

Pictured is a men's and boys' outing in the summer of 1920 in the Uinta Mountains. This is possibly a ward event for the Church of Jesus Christ of Latter-day Saints. Some traveled by horse and wagons, while others had automobiles. Note that the "road" is more of two-track trail. (Used by permission, Uintah County Library Regional History Center, all rights reserved.)

This is Wolf Creek Pass, when it was still a meandering dirt road, near the western edge of the Uinta Mountains. The picture is undated but was possibly taken in the 1940s. Today, Wolf Creek Pass (U-35) is a 21-mile-long, paved road from Woodland to Stockmore. It is famous for its wildflowers and wildlife. (Used by permission, Uintah County Library Regional History Center, all rights reserved.)

The O. Anderson family, with seven people, camps in the Uinta Mountains in August 1929. Note the two youngest children posing patiently for the photograph, while the rest of the family seems intent on preparing for a meal. (Courtesy of J. Willard Marriott Digital Library, the University of Utah.)

This 1912 picture shows a typical US Forest Service ranger camping in northern Utah. Note the simplicity of the tent being used. The tent is tall but not very wide. The ranger appears to be cooking breakfast. Since there are two horses in the background, there may be two rangers camping here, and the second one may have taken the photograph. (Courtesy of the US Forest Service.)

Pictured from left to right, Freda Davis and Muriel Wallace, both of Vernal, Utah, stand in a forest in the Uinta Mountains, The picture is undated, but it might be from the 1950s. Note that the two women are both wearing dresses, a more common occurrence back then than today in a forest. (Used by permission, Uintah County Library Regional History Center, all rights reserved.)

Cabins at the Moon Lake Resort are shown in this photograph, possibly from the 1930s. Sitting under aspen trees are four cabins and the main lodge of that era. Moon Lake is located 32 miles north of the town of Duchesne, and the resort dates back to 1927. (Used by permission, Uintah County Library Regional History Center, all rights reserved.)

People listen to a discussion in an amphitheater at Moon Lake on August 21, 1940. This was reported to be the first Uintah Basin Educational Short Course. Approximately 1,000 people attended that three-day encampment. Note the piano sitting among the aspen trees. (Used by permission, Uintah County Library Regional History Center, all rights reserved.)

Two young boys fish and enjoy the reflective view on the east side of Mirror Lake in the High Uintas. This photograph, likely from the 1940s, shows Bald Mountain in the background. (Courtesy of Utah State Historical Society.)

A lone fisherman stands on a makeshift dock at an unidentified lake in the High Uintas, probably around 1950. With more than 1,000 lakes and half of them fishable, the Uintas are the greatest fishing haven in the state of Utah. The only downside is the short summer season at the high elevations for this bounty of lakes. (Courtesy of Utah State Historical Society.)

Fish are stocked by airplane at an unidentified lake in the High Uintas, possibly in the 1960s. Pack animals were originally used to stock fish each summer in the Uintas. However, that meant only a few lakes could be stocked each year. Starting in 1955, planes have been utilized, meaning hundreds of lakes can be stocked with trout. (Courtesy of Utah State Historical Society.)

Milton Harold "Milt" Searle enjoys a fishing and camping trip at Queant Lake in the mid-1950s. Searle was a veteran who served in the Marines and who with his brother opened a business in Vernal called Milt's Merchandise Mart. Queant Lake is located on the south slope of Uintas and requires a 12-mile round-trip hike for access. (Used by permission, Uintah County Library Regional History Center, all rights reserved.)

A man uses an inflatable raft to fish one of the Granddaddy Lakes in the High Uintas, while his female companion mans the oars. Another fisherman stands by the lakeshore. This photograph was likely taken in the 1940s. (Courtesy of Utah State Historical Society.)

These two women seem content to enjoy the mountain scenery and a deep gorge in the High Uintas, with a small stream at the bottom. The location is unidentified, though the picture was likely taken in the 1940s. (Courtesy of Utah State Historical Society.)

An unidentified woman watches her two young daughters play in the summer snow along the Mirror Lake Highway, possibly near Mirror Lake, in the early 1930s. This photograph comes from the Ray King collection. (Courtesy of Utah State Historical Society.)

Three unidentified young women explore a rustic cabin in the Uinta Mountains, sometime in the early 1970s. Whether this cabin was built by a miner or a hunter is not known, but those were the most common seasonal residents for such cabins in the late 1800s and early 1900s. (Courtesy of J. Willard Marriott Digital Library, the University of Utah.)

Barney Goodman and his son Jim of Vernal, Utah, pose with the bobcat they shot while hunting in the High Uintas on October 25, 1962. Seasonal hunting is allowed in certain portions of the Uintas. (Used by permission, Uintah County Library Regional History Center, all rights reserved.)

During the 1950s, Earl and Bessie Chivers and Norman Chivers are pictured (left to right) on a deer hunting trip with their prize. The trio hunted in the Red Cloud Loop of the Uinta Mountains. They all lived in the Vernal area. Game animals are abundant in the Uintas, but hunting is strictly regulated. (Used by permission, Uintah County Library Regional History Center, all rights reserved.)

Eight

MODERN
UINTA MOUNTAINS

The modern Uintas have become much more popular, perhaps too much so. As such, user fees are being charged more and more to access trails and facilities. The first fees for using attractions along the Mirror Lake Highway were instituted around 2005.

Highway 150, the Mirror Lake Highway, is a free scenic drive, but if one stops at any attraction, a US Forest Service fee is applicable. In 2023, the fee for one to three days of use was $6; a weekly fee, $12; and an annual pass, $45. There are some 15 campgrounds along Highway 150, or adjacent to it, plus as many trailheads.

For those who want a sample of High Uintas hiking but without extreme effort, the Bald Mountain trailhead is very popular for that. Located just off the Mirror Lake Highway, a three-mile hike leads to an 11,929-foot summit that overlooks Mirror Lake as well as a wide area of basins and lakes.

By 2001, some outdoor enthusiasts started making late winter climbs up Kings Peak in early March—and loved it. They primarily use snowshoes or cross-country skis, and the leaders have to break a sort of path in the snow for the rest to follow. Kings Peak in the summer remains a very popular hike too, especially in this modern age of "peak bagging"—conquering the highest of peaks.

For the more sedentary, there are cabins to rent at the Bear River Lodge, on the far east side of Highway 150. There are also ATVs and snowmobiles to rent in this area. In addition, there are at least two other resorts in the Uintas—Moon Lake Resort on the south end and Spirit Lake Lodge on the northeast side.

There are numerous homes to the south of Bear River Lodge as well as several Scout camps and other types of camps. There is also a summer home area on the western side of the Uintas, at Soapstone.

The Church of Jesus Christ of Latter-day Saints (LDS) even has some camps in the High Uintas. LDS stakes in Layton developed a summer camp at Lake Lyman in the 1960s.

These are some of the remains of the Jesse Knight flume and ditch in the Uinta Basin, which took water from the south slope of the Uinta Mountains for farming and ranching use. This line, built from 1913 to 1914, is indicative of innovative construction in harsh western weather conditions. (Courtesy of Library of Congress.)

This is another view of the Jesse Knight flume and ditch in the Uinta Basin. Vandalism and natural forces have destroyed the flume in some places, while other locations are in reasonable condition. Jesse Knight also started the Blue Bench Irrigation District in the area. (Courtesy of Library of Congress.)

LeAnn Arave, the author's wife, poses next to a warning sign at the base of the Bald Mountain trail in the mid-1980s. The sign instructs hikers not to climb the 11,943-foot-high mountain if any storms are visible because of the high lightning strike risk that can present. (Photograph by author.)

Portions of the central Uintas include wilderness areas where there are certain restrictions, such as no motorized vehicles or even bicycle usage. The US Forest Service has installed signs letting visitors know when they have entered a wilderness/primitive area. The wilderness designation began in 1984 and includes 460,000 acres. (Photograph by Roger Arave.)

The Mirror Lake Highway (U-150) includes this summit sign at Bald Mountain Pass. Although the actual elevation number listed here has varied somewhat over the decades, this pass has always been the highest-elevation paved highway section in the entire state of Utah. The road and pass are only open seasonally in the summer. (Photograph by author.)

The Bald Mountain hiking trail is located just a few hundred yards north of the Mirror Lake Highway, at Bald Mountain Pass. A dirt parking lot is available for dozens of vehicles. The trail is roughly 2.5 miles to the Bald Mount Summit, a 11,943-foot elevation. The elevation gain on the trail is 1,169 feet. (Photograph by author.)

An early section of the trail to Bald Mountain can still be blocked with snow well into late July, as this picture proves. The sun does not directly reach this southeast section, hence the lingering snow. Hikers can usually detour around the obstacle, and some even turn right, go straight up the snowfield, and rejoin the trail hundreds of yards later, in a shortcut. (Photograph by author.)

This is the aerial view after about a half-mile hike on the Bald Mountain trail. The trailhead's dirt parking lot is seen below. This trail is perhaps the easiest of routes to summit a nearly 12,000-foot mountain in Utah. The trail is fairly well defined and is suitable for children, with adult supervision. (Photograph by author.)

This spacious view is looking southwest from the trail to Bald Mountain. The Mirror Lake Highway is shown below, as it gradually snakes through the landscape and up toward the pass. The lower Uinta Mountains are seen in the distance, looking westward toward the distant Wasatch Mountains. (Photograph by author.)

This photograph was taken about two-thirds of the way to the Bald Mountain summit. The view is to the northwest and shows the Wasatch Mountains of Davis and Weber Counties looming far in the distance. Note the increase in vegetation as the elevation decreases in the Uinta Mountains. (Photograph by author.)

A trio of hikers, (pictured from left to right) Roger and Taylor Arave and Liz Arave Hafen, pause and converse along the Bald Mountain trail at a rock cairn, strategically placed to mark the correct path. Hiking from here involves the final climb to the summit of Bald Mountain. (Photograph by author.)

The summit of Bald Mountain provides one of the most panoramic views in the entire Uinta Mountains. Note the thick forest in the lower valleys of the High Uintas versus the rugged, barren peaks encircling them. Clouds are common most summer days in the Uintas, as almost every day has at least a slight chance of precipitation. (Photograph by Roger Arave.)

Hayden Peak is spotlighted at center in this view from atop Bald Mountain, looking northeast. Hayden Peak is a 12,479-foot mountain that features a long, butte-like top adorned with a single, small bump for an actual summit. Note the Mirror Lake Highway looping through the valley below. (Photograph by Roger Arave.)

Mirror Lake, perhaps the most popular geographical feature in the High Uintas, is seen in this aerial view from near the top of Bald Mountain. The east side of Bald Mountain offers spectacular bird's-eye views of the lake. Even the campgrounds and paths around the lake are visible from here. (Photograph by Roger Arave.)

Roger Arave stands atop the Bald Mountain summit, 11,943 feet above sea level. The mountaintop is marked by a small rock cairn. Hayden Peak, Kletting Peak, and others are readily visible in this picture. One standard feature of most High Uinta Mountain peaks is the many slabs of flat rock that dominate the tops of the summits. (Photograph by Roger Arave.)

This is a view of the narrow trail to Bald Mountain as it switchbacks up the steep hillside. There are many loose, small rocks in this area, and there is also evidence of significant erosion. Note that there is some sparse vegetation along the mountainside as the temperatures get cooler the higher the trail ascends. (Photograph by Roger Arave.)

The east side of the Wasatch Mountains in Salt Lake County are readily visible in the background along the trail to Bald Mountain. The extra tall Wasatch Peaks to the south are likely the American Fork Twin Peaks, above Snowbird ski resort. The mountain on the far left side of the picture may be Timpanogos Peak in Utah County. (Photograph by Roger Arave.)

This is a close-up picture of a rock cairn in the Uinta Mountains. These piles of rock are very common and used as both a courtesy and a safety feature to keep hikers on the correct path. They are also often located on the top of a summit, as a sort of monument and to remove any doubt as to the highest point around the area. (Photograph by author.)

This is a view from the Bald Mountain trail, with Mirror Lake visible below. Bald Mountain Pass separates drainages in the High Uintas. The Weber and Provo River drainages are on the west side of Bald Mountain. The Duchesne River, Bear River, and other drainages are on the east side of the pass. (Photograph by Roger Arave.)

A hiking group descends from upper Henry's Fork after hiking to Kings Peak. The High Uintas offer a wealth of endurance running and hiking opportunities—and all of it in rarified air. Kings Peak is visible in the center of the picture, appearing almost like a sinking ship. (Photograph by Ravell Call.)

Kings Peak, center, rises like a sinking ship on the horizon from the top of Henry's Fork Basin. Also visible is Anderson Pass and the rockslide shortcut to Kings Peak. Henry's Fork is the most popular route today to Kings Peak. In the past, hikers would ascend to Kings Peak via Gunsight Pass. However, today, the rockslide shortcut is most commonly used, as it climbs right below Anderson Pass. (Photograph by Ravell Call.)

Author Lynn Arave slowly hikes along the lower edge of Andersons Pass, elevation 12,703 feet, on the way to Kings Peak, elevation 13,528 feet. Perhaps the hardest segment of hiking to Kings Peak is ascending out of Henry's Fork Basin and onto the ridgeline as that is the steepest section. (Photograph by Ravell Call.)

Scott Wesemann (left) and Roger Arave (right) scramble slowly up the shortcut toward the top of Andersons Pass in the Uinta Mountains. The steep and rocky Anderson Pass route saves time and distance but is slow going. Ideally, hikers summit Kings Peak by late morning or early afternoon to avoid the threat of lightning storms. (Photograph by author.)

Scott Wesemann (left) nears the top of the rockslide shortcut on the way to Kings Peak from Henry's Fork Basin. Once hikers leave the basin, they trek entirely over loose rock slabs and boulders to Kings Peak. Hiking poles can be a very helpful tool for these uneven and rocky areas. Roger Arave (right) follows behind. (Photograph by Ravell Call.)

Pictured is the top of Kings Peak in early August 1990. Back then, hikers often had the entire mountaintop to themselves. When "peak bagging" became popular a decade later, it was common on most summer days to find a dozen or more hikers sharing the peak. (Photograph by author.)

This is the original metal plaque that used to adorn Kings Peak. It is shown here in 1990. The sign was installed by the US Forest Service, likely in the 1970s. However, by the early 2000s, the sign was missing and apparently never found. It is believed that someone pried it loose from the rock it was attached to, stole it, or perhaps threw it over the cliff. (Photograph by author.)

Kings Peak is shown in the distance from Henry's Fork Basin. With plenty of trees and lakes, the basin is a popular camping location for those who hike to Kings Peak in multiday backpacking trips. In fact, Dollar Lake (not shown) is the most popular camping spot in the area. (Photograph by Ravell Call.)

This is the view from the mountain saddle, below Kings Peak, peering north into Henry's Fork Basin. Note the sheer cliff to the left and the aptly named Cliff Lake at the bottom. The High Uintas are the epitome of rugged alpine scenery and live up to the name "Rocky Mountains." (Photograph by Ravell Call.)

This is a close-up photograph of the south side of Kings Peak in 1990. South Kings Peak, the state's second-tallest summit, is visible to the right and behind the mound. Until 1966, South Kings Peak was erroneously believed to be the state's highest peak, and hikers would skirt by today's Kings Peak, oblivious to its 16-foot-higher elevation. (Photograph by author.)

This view from Kings Peak shows South Kings Peak (second-tallest summit in Utah) from the north side. On this August afternoon, about a dozen hikers (some of them Boy Scouts) were sitting on Kings Peak. Note how rugged the edge of Kings Peak appears, as seen at lower left. (Photograph by Ravell Call.)

Looking north, this is how Kings Peak, elevation 13,528 feet, appears while standing atop South Kings Peak. Kings Peak has a much smaller top and appears far less stable than its counterpart to the south. Even so, Kings Peak is 16 feet higher than South Kings Peak. (Photograph by Ravell Call.)

Erosion has altered the landscape in the High Uintas over the eons. This is the view looking west from near the top of Gilbert Peak down a ravine below the summit. This rugged gully has become one of the most common routes to climb to Gilbert Peak from Henry's Fork Basin below. (Photograph by Ravell Call.)

Seemingly endless boulders fields and slabs of rock comprise the "roof of Utah" in the High Uintas. There are no smooth hiking paths here, but if one needs a rock to rest on, there are countless choices. This view is from the western edge of Gilbert Peak. (Photograph by Ravell Call.)

This is how Kings Peak and South Kings Peak (center) appear from Gilbert Peak, elevation 13,449 feet. Gilbert Peak is more than 60 feet shorter than Kings Peak and South Kings Peak and as only the third-tallest summit in the Uintas is often climbed less. There is also a far less defined path to the Gilbert summit. (Photograph by Ravell Call.)

This is a view of the Gilbert Peak summit. It boasts a very wide and rocky summit. A US Geological Survey marker is also shown in the picture. Note the rocky niche where many an exhausted hiker has likely found a little shelter from elements. (Photograph by Ravell Call.)

This is a close-up photograph of the US Geological Survey marker atop Gilbert Peak. These markers are routinely cemented at the top of key mountain summits. Gilbert Peak was named for Grove Karl Gilbert, a geologist in government expeditions of the 1870s in Utah Territory and the western states. (Photograph by Ravell Call.)

This photograph, from August 2003, shows Ravell Call atop Gilbert Peak. Call and Craig Lloyd were able to hike to the state's three highest summits in the Uinta Mountains in a single day, a rare feat. Camping at Dollar Lake, they ascended Kings Peak first, then South Kings Peak, and finally Gilbert Peak before returning to base camp the same day. (Courtesy of Ravell Call.)

This is one of the bear warning signs in the High Uintas. Black bears reside there, and keeping a clean camp and food out of reach of bears are good policies to have. If one encounters a bear, yell, throw rocks, wave both arms, and slowly retreat, walking backwards. Do not make eye contact. (Photograph by author.)

This is an informational sign about the Boreal toads in the High Uintas. The Utah Division of Wildlife Resources wants outdoor users to watch for them but not to pick them up, as they are endangered. Contact the Utah Division of Wildlife Resources if one is spotted and maybe take pictures and note the location. These toads live in many western states and western Canada. (Photograph by author.)

This photograph, from the summer of 2009, shows the aftermath of a forest fire, several years earlier, in the Bear River watershed. Despite its high elevation, forest fires in the Uintas are still a hazard. Campers need to be extremely careful with their campfires and make sure they are completely extinguished. (Photograph by author.)

Hikers walk through the aftermath of the East Fork of the Bear River Fire, which occurred in June 2002. This fire scorched 14,000 acres in the Uintas and cost more than $13 million in firefighting expenditures. Despite fire restrictions being in place, a group of youth camping in the area lit fires and they were left unattended, causing the blaze. (Photograph by author.)

Frolicking is a popular pastime, especially among the youth at Mirror Lake. Here, Taylor Arave wades in the shallow waters at the shoreline. Note how clear the water is. The water temperature of lakes in the High Uintas is always very cold, though, and swimming is not recommended. (Photograph by author.)

Nothing beats the beauty of summer wildflowers at high elevations. This August 2013 photograph shows Elle Arave playing in the flowers, in the meadows near Mirror Lake. Another popular place for wildflowers is at Ruth's Lake, a little farther up the Mirror Lake Highway. At the Pass Lake trailhead, a 0.8-mile hike is required to reach Ruth's Lake. (Photography by Whitney Arave.)

This photograph shows the remains of an old wooden cabin in the High Uintas, next to a trail. It is likely either from the mining era of the area or from a rancher before the Uintas had wilderness designation. Elevation here is about 10,000 feet above sea level. (Photograph by author.)

Pictured is Mirror Lake around 2015. A foot trail circles the entire lake. There is a seven-day limit for staying at the lake's campground. The campground includes pit toilets, drinking water, and picnic tables. There is also a boat ramp, but no motorized boats are permitted there. ATVS are not permitted either. (Photograph by author.)

This is a photograph of where the Bear River crosses eastward under Highway 150, just past the Wyoming-Utah state line. This sign is in Wyoming, just past the edge of the Uinta Mountains. The Bear River eventually flows into the Great Salt Lake and is that lake's main tributary. (Photograph by author.)

This picture shows the exact point where the left-hand fork and the right-hand fork of the Bear River combine into a single waterway. Below The Cathedral mountain and at an elevation of around 9,350 feet, the two streams join to create what first appears on maps as the Bear River. (Technically, it is the river's east fork.) No fanfare at this junction, not even a footbridge across the Bear River on the trail here, just more rushing water. (Photograph by author.)

Following the left-hand fork of the Bear River upward leads to an impressive falls/cascade at an elevation of 9,535 feet. When this photograph was taken on a late July afternoon, the air temperature was only about 68 degrees there. The water temperature was much cooler, at only about 39 degrees. (Photograph by author.)

This is another photograph of the long cascade of the left-hand fork of the Bear River down The Cathedral mountain to where it joins with the right-hand fork. The Bear River travels some 300 miles from the Uintas before it empties into the Great Salt Lake. The Bear River is the longest flowing US river that does not dump into an ocean. (Photograph by author.)

This is a picture of the west end of the Duchesne Tunnel, a six-mile-long conduit that takes water from the east side of the Uinta Mountains and transfers it into the Provo River drainage on the west side. This tunnel can be viewed along a very short footpath off the Mirror Lake Highway. (Photograph by Roger Arave.)

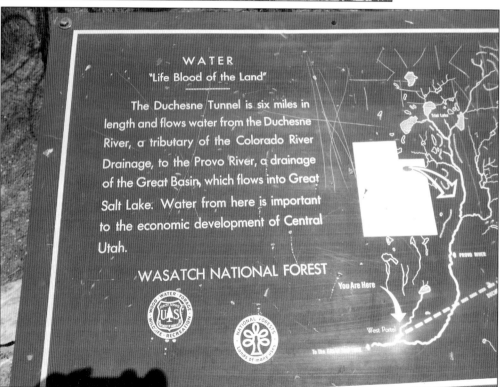

This is the commemorative sign that heralds the west end of the Duchesne Tunnel. This sign is located about 21 miles east of Kamas, along the path that leads to a view of the west end of the tunnel. The concrete-lined tunnel, completed in 1954, is 10 feet in diameter. (Photograph by author.)

The Provo River Falls overlook is one of the main highlights along the Mirror Lake Highway (U-150). From Kamas, the overlook is 23.5 miles eastward. The elevation here is 9,300 feet above sea level. There is a parking lot and a marked trail. A close-up view of the falls requires negotiating a series of stairs. (Photograph by author.)

This Provo River Falls, a highlight in the area since pioneer times, is shown here. This picture was taken in late July during a dry period, when the flow of the falls was on the low side. Some visitors like to wade below the waterfalls, which appear to flow down a series of natural, rock "stairs." (Photograph by Roger Arave.)

This is a typical trail/lake wooden directional sign in the High Uintas. With more than 1,000 natural lakes and some heavily forested areas, signs are as much a safety feature as they are a convenience to trail users. From the East Fork Bear River trailhead, the distance is nine miles to Allsop Lake. (Photograph by author.)

This is a typical meadow during the summer season in the High Uintas. This one is in the Bear River drainage. Note the dead trees in the area too. Various blights over the decades have killed trees in forests of the western United States. Meadows are often a prime place to sometimes run into moose. (Photograph by author.)

This is a photograph of Reid's Peak, with an 11,708-foot elevation. Located northwest of Bald Mountain, this is how this distinctive peak appears from the west end of the Bald Mountain trail. It is rarely climbed, though, as it only involves a five-mile, round-trip trek. Most hikers favor the taller peaks in the area instead. (Photograph by author.)

A group of hikers traverse one of the countless meadows in the Uinta Mountains. Cloudless days are not very common in the High Uintas. Clouds often thicken in the early afternoon and can pose a threat of rain and thunderstorms. Lightning strikes are a key danger here. (Photograph by Roger Arave.)

In 2003, author Lynn Arave (left) and his son Roger (right) set up their tent at a camping area near Dollar Lake in the Henry's Fork area of the High Uintas. Henry's Fork contains several good fishing lakes, and Dollar Lake is a popular halfway mark for those hiking to Kings Peak. (Photograph by Ravell Call.)

This is a typical summer campground in the High Uintas during the 1980s. The family has everything they need—a tent trailer, a campfire pit, picnic table, and a shady area. Shelter is always a wise idea in the High Uintas, where brief afternoon thunderstorms are more common than totally dry days. (Photograph by author.)

LeAnn Arave poses with her son Roger during the summer of 1988 at Mirror Lake, elevation 10,500 feet above sea level. Besides the much cooler temperatures in the High Uintas, the rugged mountain scenery in the area is spectacular. The Arave family had to drive just two hours from Davis County to reach Mirror Lake. (Photograph by author.)

This is a photograph of the boat dock at Lake Lyman, a camp by the Layton, Utah, stakes of the Church of Jesus Christ of Latter-day Saints. The camp began decades ago with a 99-year lease from the US Forest Service. It is located near Elizabeth Mountain. (Photograph by LeAnn Arave.)

Three unidentified young women canoe on Lake Lyman, probably in 2009. Lake Lyman covers 27 acres and has a maximum depth of 20 feet. It is located at an elevation of 9,700 feet in the Blacks Fork drainage, on the east slope of the Uintas. Little Lake Lyman as well as a few other small lakes are also in the same area. (Photograph by Liz Arave Hafen.)

Three hikers slowly climb up the Lofty Lake Trail to the pass between Lofty and Scout Peaks. This four-mile trail begins at Scout Lake, near Camp Steiner. (Steiner is the highest-elevation Boy Scout camp in the nation at 10,400 feet.) The trail offers stunning views of the area as well as several good fishing opportunities. (Photograph by author.)

Roger Arave takes a high-altitude rest break along the upper reaches of the Lofty Lake Trail in the Uinta Mountains. This location featured an amazingly flat, rocky area. Mirror Lake can be seen in the distance. This trail is one of the most popular paths along the Mirror Lake Highway. (Photograph by author.)

Author Lynn Arave stands atop one of the highest points along the Lofty Lake Trail in the High Uintas during a 1995 hike with family members. This view is looking north into Wyoming. Moose sightings are common along the northern section of the Lofty Lake Trail. (Photograph by Roger Arave.)

Roger Arave poses along the upper portion of the Lofty Lake Trail in the summer of 1995. Elevation here is around 11,400 feet above sea level. The four-mile-long trail passes by three lakes—Scout, Lofty, and Kamas—and climbs a total of 1,000 feet in elevation. (Photograph by author.)

Taylor Arave fishes at Teapot Lake in the summer of 2009. This lake is just off Highway 150 and one mile east of Trial Lake. Teapot Lake covers 14 acres and is up to 51 feet deep. Camping is very popular around the lake, which drains into the Provo River. (Photograph by Roger Arave.)

A dog looks down into Wall Lake during a 1985 hike. The high and steep banks around this lake are enhanced by a manmade dam. This lake is now as large as 61 acres in size and up to 128 feet deep because of the enlargement work a century ago that made it into a reservoir. A hike to Wall Lake is just 2.5 miles round-trip and begins at the Crystal Lake trailhead. (Photograph by author.)

The High Uintas are not just comprised of rocky, talus slopes. There is considerable forest throughout the Uinta Mountains too. This dense forest view is just below the plateau where the headwaters of the Bear River originate. Visitors and backpackers are advised to check for restrictions on firewood and campfires before leaving into the wilderness. (Photograph by Roger Arave.)

KLETTING PEAK
(ELEVATION 12,000 FEET)

NAMED FOR RICHARD K.A. KLETTING (1858-1943), EMINENT ARCHITECT, WHO DESIGNED UTAH'S CAPITOL AND OTHER PROMINENT BUILDINGS. KLETTING ALSO DEVOTED HIS LIFE TO PIONEERING IN CONSERVATION. IN 1897 HE SPONSORED THE DESIGNATION OF THESE HIGH UINTA MOUNTAINS AS THE FIRST FOREST RESERVE IN UTAH, FOR THEIR RESOURCES IN TIMBER, RANGE, WILDLIFE, WATERSHED, AND RECREATION.

This is the metal plaque that commemorates the name of Kletting Peak, with a 12,000-foot elevation. It is found along Highway 150, six miles northeast of Mirror Lake, on the east side of the highway and below Kletting Peak itself. Ample signage highlights the monument's location. The peak was named Kletting in 1964, and the monument has been there ever since. (Photograph by Roger Arave.)

BIBLIOGRAPHY

Deseret News archives
en.wikipedia.org, Uinta Mountains
Gates, John L. *Lakes of the High Uintas.* Utah State Division of Fish and Game, 1964.
historytogo.utah.gov, A History of Utah's American Indians
indian.utah.gov, Ute Indian Tribe of the Uinta & Ouray Reservation
Standing, A.R. "Through the Uintas: History of the Carter Road." *Utah Historical Quarterly*, Vol. 35, No. 3, 1967.
Utah Digital Newspapers, digitalnewspapers.org
Van Cott, John W. *Utah Place Names.* Salt Lake City: University of Utah Press, 1990.
www.newspapers.com
www.usgs.gov, The Geologic Story of the Uinta Mountains
www.utah.com, Uinta Mountains

Discover Thousands of Local History Books Featuring Millions of Vintage Images

Arcadia Publishing, the leading local history publisher in the United States, is committed to making history accessible and meaningful through publishing books that celebrate and preserve the heritage of America's people and places.

Find more books like this at
www.arcadiapublishing.com

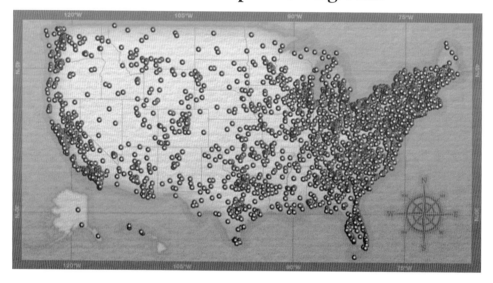

Search for your hometown history, your old stomping grounds, and even your favorite sports team.

Consistent with our mission to preserve history on a local level, this book was printed in South Carolina on American-made paper and manufactured entirely in the United States. Products carrying the accredited Forest Stewardship Council (FSC) label are printed on 100 percent FSC-certified paper.

MADE IN THE USA